Hey, God!

Hey, God!

Side-splittingly Funny Letters to God

Kip Conlon

**Andrews McMeel
Publishing**

Kansas City

Hey, God! Side-splittingly Funny Letters to God

02 03 04 05 06 CTP 10 9 8 7 6 5 4 3 2 1

Library of Congress Cataloging-in-Publication Data
Conlon, Kip.
 Hey, God! : side-splittingly funny letters to God / Kip Conlon
    p. cm.
 ISBN 0-7407-2690-0
    1. God—Humor. 2. Conduct of life—Humor. I. Title.
PN6231.P3 C65 2002
816'.6—dc21   2002019797

Book design: Holly Camerlinck
Illustrations: Susan Conlon

Hey, Reader:
An Introduction

The following letters were gathered in response to an informal study done in various universities, libraries, rest homes, churches, museums, movie theatres, town halls, malls, mosques, car dealerships, etc. Throughout the country, anywhere adults congregated, we tried to be there. The purpose of this study was simple: to see if we could turn a profit selling a book just like those kids' letters to God books, except with the word "adults" where "kids" used to be. Our hope was that we could.

And why not? Why should kids have all the fun? Are they the only ones with cutesy questions for our Creator? Or poignant, profound observations about our existence and role in the universe? We weren't sure.

That's also why we did the study. We're still not sure. But we got a lot of letters on the cheap, enough to fill a book, as a matter of fact. "Call a publisher!" someone shouted. The rest, as they say, is history. Enjoy.

Incidentally, if anyone reading this has had a near-death experience they'd like documented for time immemorial, we were thinking of slapping together a book of those for our next venture. We hear that's where the big bucks are. Write care of the publisher.

— Kip Conlon, Ed.

SAM STERN

Dear God:

I went to church this Sunday and the minister mentioned over and over Your "plan" for each and every one of us. I was wondering if You really had a plan for me, and if so, what was my marriage to Linda all about?

Yours truly,

Sam Stern

(age 44)

Dear God:

Please please please please
don'T leT Marisa be pregnanT.
   I will be really, really good
from here on in and give loTs
of dough To chariTy.

Thank you.

Sincerely,
Dave

(age 26)

Dear God:

You know my girlfriend, Stephanie? The other night she left her e-mail open on the computer and there, without really meaning to look, I saw this weird message from some "Mark" about how Saturday "meant more to [him] than she could know." Saturday's when I took my brother out for his birthday and she said she felt really tired.

What's that thing you do, "smiting"? Could you maybe smite this guy Mark? And also make Stephanie love me again, but I asked you that before and she hasn't yet, FYI.

Sorry to pester you,

Demetri

(age 34)

Dear God:

How is heaven today? Things are pretty slow here in Lansing, but it sure is sunny, and thanks for that.

i did as you commanded when you appeared to me in the form of Cyril, my hamster, and instructed me to shoot my parents in their sleep with the shotgun that appeared in my sock drawer. Weird, their being agents of the devil like You/Cyril said, though it makes a lot of sense, looking back.

Awaiting instruction on what to do with the corpses.

Your Servant,

John Ray Ebberly

(age 28)

C. B. MᶜCLAIN

Dear God:

I am a corporation lawyer for a company that if I told you the name you'd know it right away. As you in your Infinite Wisdom have guessed, I am extremely wealthy. Really just a note to say thanks, Big Guy.

Life's been good, to say the least. The kids, the enormous house, the trophy wife, the nubile mistress. True, there's been a profusion of Italians as of late in our gated community, but they seem, as Italians go, good ones. (I'd take an Italian over a straight-up Hispanic any day.) Keep up the G.W.

Cordially,

(age 54)

Dear ~~God~~:

Thank you for helping me
to stop peeing in my bed!
The sheets are funner to lie
in when they are unwet!
You no that enz you are
~~God~~! Say hi to ~~Jesus~~!

Louise

(age 77)

Dear God:

I am a Catholic, but I'm also a strict vegetarian. Should I be taking communion?

Could perhaps a vegetarian alternative be supplied for people in my predicament? Maybe a soy body of Christ?

Drinking blood's probably a no-no, now that I think of it. I'll give Gary at Healthy Pleasures a call, see what he has to say.

Torn in Tarzana,

Michael

(age 25)

Dear God:

My big-shot brother, Dale, who's really religious, always used to say how You work "in mysterious ways." Then he fell off his roof and impaled himself on his picket fence while fetching my niece's Frisbee. He sure didn't see that coming.

Now I sleep with his wife in his big warm house, drive his Lexus, and my niece calls me "Daddy."

Dale sure was right.

George

(age 44)

Dear God:

I wonder if by now Jesus is talking to Judas. I bet if he is it's still pretty awkward and tense. Where Judas is overly friendly and always opening doors and trying to pay for everything and Jesus is, of course, polite but feels like he wants to say, "Relax, Judas."

Ann Myers

(age 42)

Dear God:

Faithful servant Pastor Childriss here.

In my 20+ years presiding over Your flock at St. Mark's in Selville, I think You'd agree I've been pretty good about resisting temptation. So much so, some might suggest you might have stopped sending it my way by now. Which brings me to the parishioner Angela McKeever. Let me just say, Lord, as someone who's a longtime fan of your work to begin with: Wow!

Anyway, I thought I'd give You a heads-up that I might flunk this particular little test. I have sinned in my heart, Lord, and if all goes well after the bake sale on Saturday, I will soon sin with other parts of my body.

Really sorry about this,

Evan

(age 41)

Dear God:

"It's a Wonderful Life" was on tonight. I imagine you really like that movie. I tried to think what the world would be like if I'd never been born. I couldn't really see that big a difference.

I also thought how everyone would have been much better off if Uncle Billy had never been born. He's the one who screws up everything. But then, where's your movie?

Joe

(age 53)

Dear God:

Please let Mommy and Daddy talk to each other again then fall in love again and get married again and we can all live together in Seattle like a happy family like before again.

Please?

Joyce

(age 36)

Dear God:

What do you think of the new JESUS IS MY BEST FRIEND bumper sticker on the Honda? Sometimes I think it's sort of weird. Like, "Why am I telling this to people?"

Stephen

(age 27)

JESUS
is my best friend

Dear God:

Maybe You were aware of this, but Frank and I have made up the guest room for Your Boy should He ever come down again. It's the best room in the house, if You ask me, and Frank Junior'll tell You the same thing, and then some.

Please forgive Frank Junior. He's just tired of the attic. It does get pretty drafty—can't say as how I blame him. In terms of visits, I was thinking March might be nice.

Yours truly,
Emma Crowley

(age 46)

Dear God:

I was thinking about when Jesus rose Lazarus from the dead. They never mention when he dies the second time. I bet when he did there was ten minutes or so when everyone was looking around to see if Jesus'd show up to save the day again.

Some people are never satisfied.

Sincerely,
Matt

(age 30)

Youngstown, Ohio

Dear God,

I imagine heaven as a lot like France. I've never been to France. I've never been to heaven, either!

I imagine if there is a hell, it's a lot like Youngstown, Ohio.

Amy

(age 23)

Dear God:

I was, I must admit, pretty rude to that guy at the door just now, the one with all the literature and the short-sleeve dress shirt with the pocketful of pens who talked about your glory.

I'm sorry, I shouldn't have snapped like that.

The game was tied, Sosa at the plate, bottom of the eighth, I'm just sitting down again, the doorbell rings, it was not a great moment.

Please forgive me and I pray for, I think his name was Robert, to have a great day and better luck at the other condos.

Mike McGill

(age 41)

Dear God:

It is Christmas. My girlfriend left me. If you want to give me a present you could give me her. Her name's Jordan. You know her.

I had like four beers before I wrote this. I don't usually believe in you.

No offense.

Your pal,
Bob

(age 27)

Dear God:

The doctors told me I died on the table for a minute. For a minute I was dead! They made a lot of jokes about it, but I didn't see what was so funny.

I thought for sure there'd be a light, or angels, or I didn't know what all, but all I remember seeing was that one nurse with the not-great skin saying, "Welcome back!" when I woke up.

Everyone's a comedian.

Well, just wanted to say, good to still be here, and maybe next time when there's more time, someone can show me around the place.

Dan Carles

(age 64)

Dear God,

I talked to Father Troiano this afternoon about the church's attitude toward premarital sex. I was not very surprised when he informed me they are not all for it. So I'm going over his head here, God.

    I really like Alphonse, and am sure I will marry him eventually. He already sort of asked me. So if it's all right with You, the you-know, please show me a sign such as making it rain sometime this month.

Yours truly,

Agnes

(age 28)

Dear God,

Everyone's pretty pissed off at me right now. I got really

drunk at that party at Tim's and I guess was kind of hitting

on Erica, Tim's girlfriend. At least that's how it seemed to

Tim. And Erica. And Kerry, my girlfriend. I don't expect

you to do anything about it or anything. I just needed a

friend.

Rob

(age 24)

Dear God,

Hi. I am shy when it comes to what my dad called, "the fairer sex" (girls). Anyway, I would like one and I am not picky because I figure who I get would have to not be picky also on account of I am not much to look at and not some big success.

Just to throw out some ideas, I think I would love the woman in Apartment 4A and vice versa, if she got to know me. Her name, I think, is Anna.

I pray for you to help me in this matter.

Love,
Dom

(age 44)

Dear God,

My dad once let it slip he and Mom didn't mean to make me, I was an "accident." By "once let it slip," I mean he said it anytime I did anything mildly displeasing, such as leaving my bike out in the rain or handing him a Pepsi when he asked for a Coke.

Anyway, apart from large chunks of my childhood, I sure have enjoyed your planet and its people. I hope me and my kind have not disrupted events by crashing the party, so to speak.

I particularly enjoy your macadamia nuts.

Sincerely,
Albert Gill

(age 52)

Dear God,

Saw on the TV some footage of that hurricane you sent up the coast. You looked awfully upset about something.

Trish was worried about her folks, who, as You know, live in Charleston. In fact, they were fine.

Better luck next time.

Yours truly,

Hank

(age 46)

LAS VEGAS, NEVADA

God—
23 black. 23 black. 23 black.

John

(age 42)

Dear God,

They had the MTV movie awards on TV last night. Will Smith gave a "shout out" to You. I guess You guys are pretty chummy, Your both being celebrities and everything.

You could consider this my little shout out.

Alyssum

(age 26)

Dear God,

Apparently, I am created in Your image. Which is
bad news for both of us, I'm afraid.

Ronald

(age 38)

Dear God,

The actor from that angel show came in tonight. He was a real jerk, he was kind of shouting at his girlfriend, sent the soup back twice, and ended up tipping me 4 percent. It sort of shook my faith, either in you or in television, I couldn't tell which.

Jess

(age 22)

Dear God,

Well, You know how everything's been going. Not great. Courtney, the job, this thing with the audit, and, oh yeah, did I mention Courtney? Usually, I'd just leave it up to one of Your earthly messengers, but "every cloud has a silver lining" isn't cutting it, thanks so much, anyway, Father Ron. Is that even true? Do clouds have linings? Are they silver? If so, why is that a good thing? For all I know, silver linings are burning holes in the ozone. And is it darkest before the dawn (again, Mr. Originality, Padre Ron)? I mean, I know it is at some point, but right before? Anyway, hour of need time. Please. Do that thing You do.

Andy

(age 39)

Dear God,

When it rains, are you crying? When the sun shines, does that mean you are happy? When the thunder claps, are you mad? When it snows—well, what's going on there? Are you crying and it's cold?

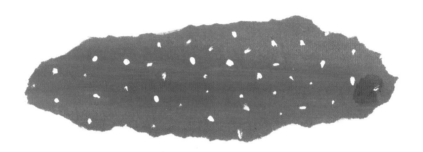

Did you trip and spill some snow you had lying around? Do you have dandruff? Eczema? Is it like some kind of pest control and you're trying to kill everyone who lives in Buffalo?

Reva

(age 41)

Dear God,

The world is sad sometimes. I think you should do something about that, to make it less sad. Because who likes to be sad? Nobody, that's who.

I will help by wearing bright colors and decorating my desk with rainbows and unicorns and by being nicer to everyone, with the exception of Roger, from the mailroom. I'm sorry but I can't stand that jerk.

Thanx and have a wonderful day!

Joy Kerney

(age 36)

Dear God,

Still stranded on the island (note the ash handwriting smeared on palm leaf). Never thought this really happened except in Bugs Bunny cartoons. Anyway, in case you haven't caught my daily screaming, I could sure use a rescue ship right about now. Or plane. I'm not choosy.

Tom Avery

(age ?)

Dear God,

Well, with this tax evasion thing, I guess the jig is pretty much up. What can I say? In Your Infinite Wisdom You made the camera love me and I was just so good at preaching, a TV ministry seemed the way to go.

If You could see fit to having me do my stay at one of these country club prisons You hear so much about, I'd be much obliged.

Technically, I spread Your Word and everything.

Yours in Christ,

Don Cooley

The Reverend Don Cooley

(age 53)

Dear God,

So I coveted my neighbor's wife, had a cup of coffee with her, then committed adultery. Whoops!

Come Judgment Day I think this should count as only one commandment, since I pretty much had to covet her first.

Maybe you take a different view.

See you soon.

Charlie

(age 30)

Dear God,

Found some magazines in Max's sock drawer—<u>those</u> kinds of magazines. It sure would be nice if You could show him the sinfulness of it. It's a conversation I really don't feel like having.

Yours truly,
Julia Morphew

(age 37)

P.S. Who does he think puts his socks in his sock drawer, anyway?

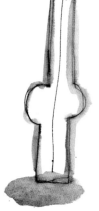

JULIA MORPHEW

Dear God,

There seemed to be a lot more miracles back in the olden times, like with Moses and that thing and that other guy and all the stuff he did. I think if you started them up again you'd be a lot more popular. Like a flying guy or a talking cat. Those are just off the top of my head.

Rick

(age 31)

Dear God,

What about reincarnation?

I ask cause sometimes I'll be watching a nature special and I'll feel this weird attraction to antelopes. Was I once an antelope?

You're really the only one I can talk to about this.

Dale Carver

(age 50)

Dear God,

CC'ing you re: this afternoon's confession. I had Father Strausburger in the booth, who doesn't hear so hot. Sins for the week of March 8: three impure thoughts, six taking-Your-name-in-vains, and I envied my brother in-law's barbecue.

Oh, and on the drive home I flipped off some lady who pulled out in front of me. What would that fall under, exactly?

In any case, I confess.

Amen,
Steve Tiggs

(age 34)

Dear God,

Joy again. Please forgive everyone in the office for their treatment of me. They know not what they do. David is just insecure because he is so stupid and scared someone will find out and he won't be supervisor anymore. And Holly is just trying to get attention, finding fault with my BLS reports, the same reason she dresses like such a slut. I'm sorry, but she does. And Roger, well, do whatever you want with Roger.

Thanx and have a super day!

Joy Kerney

(age 36)

Rodney
Kurtz

Dear God,

As you know, I am not a religious person, nor have I sought your help in the past. A typical human, I was stubborn and vain, and thought I could get along without your Sacred Grace and Divinity. I repent the error of my ways.

This Thursday's the softball championship against the Bennigan's team. I humbly invoke your help in schooling their sorry asses. That one bartender needs to go down. You know which one I mean.

Your Servant,

Rodney Kurtz

(age 23)

Dear God,

Kind of sort of accidentally wiped out the Andersen file on the shared drive. Looks like it's back to temping for me. If You would care to maybe send an angel down in the form of a tech support guy, I would just be so grateful. The dental plan is really good here.

Lindsay Jeng

(age 24)

Dear God,

It's 3:32 in the morning. Can't sleep. Again. You're up, at least. I wish we could play cards or something. Well, there's always the TV. Oh, great, *Cannonball Run II* is on. Finally, I can get the answers to all those nagging questions I had after seeing the original. Maybe I'll read. If I feel like this, how beat you must be. 3:34.

Len

(age 46)

Dear God,

Laura had the baby! A seven-pound, nine-ounce little girl!
   I thought we spoke about this. I wanted a boy. Is a Samantha going to break Hank Aaron's home run record? I don't think so.
   I don't really know how to talk to girls. Just ask Laura.

Dan Tonkovich

(age 32)

Dear God,

Oh wow. Where the hell am I? Who's this guy?

Lizzie's birthday. Champagne. Pam, I want you to meet Ted something. That's right. Mutual funds or something.

This is a really tacky apartment Ted something has.

Just, please, help me find my shoes, I'll atone in the taxi.

Pam

(age 27)

Dear God,

What's an eight-letter word for "Big Gulp Wine Bottle"?
Third letter R, fifth letter B, seventh letter—oh,
"Jeroboam." Of course.

   Thanks a lot.

Henry

(age 52)

Dear God,

Though I'm sure you did your best, we both know I'm not much in the looks department, yet I have this beautiful wife, Caroline, who so far as I know in eight years has never cheated on me or even mentioned the fact she could do so much better. Beautiful and classy. What a great wife I have. What a great God you are.

Josh Parr

(age 31)

Dear God,

Geez. Well, there's one more squirrel for your heavenly kingdom. I'm sorry. My VW handles like a truck. Before I could even wrench the wheel, it was just—too late. I hope, I don't know, I hope he was a bachelor squirrel, that there isn't like a whole bunch of them wondering where Daddy is. I should really just get a bike.

Alex

(age 23)

Rotgut

A DIVE IN MONONGAHELA

Dear God,

What's a nice girl like me doing in a place like This?

Georgia

(age 28)

Dear God,

I said that stuff about considering the beauty of the lilies, but my folks weren't buying it. Apparently, my lying on a sofa-bed on a bunch of potato-chip crumbs watching *Rockford Files* isn't that beautiful. I can sort of see their point. Help me get a job that doesn't totally suck like that gig at that pizza dump. Theme restaurants really make me question your existence, man.

Alex

(age 25)

Dear God,

So here i am, it's come to this. Let me tell you about another so-called lunatic, maybe you've heard of him? He, too, was perceived as a threat to a corrupt society. He also gave a lot of "crazy talks" about loving your fellow man <u>and</u> woman, and the power of forgiveness. Not unlike yours truly, he was misunderstood by a hostile populace. i wonder, did <u>he</u> cover himself in Mylar and a pith helmet to deflect the Venutian "brainbeams" that were trying (yet failing!) to destroy his soul? Nah. They probably would have mentioned it somewhere. i hope they have the rice pudding again today.

Billy Tibbs

(age 22)

Dear God,

I try to approach every situation with the idea,
"What would Jesus do?" which has been
immeasurably helpful and a great comfort.
Except not so much in singles' bars.

Ray

Dear God,

When I swore before you to, among other things, "obey" Rocky as his wife, I did not realize this promise would manifest itself almost entirely in trips to the store to buy beer. I might have answered differently.

Carin Zorn

(age 27)

Dear God,

IT's a parTy, I'm chaTTing nice wiTh The hosTess, I
should worry The dip mighT be made from a lobsTer?
I should inTerrupT The flow of a pleasanT
conversaTion To ask The nice lady if she's kepT kosher
wiTh The appeTizers? When someone complimenTs
her on The lobsTer dip, I should spiT whaT's in my
mouTh inTo a napkin? Like I know whaT lobsTer
TasTes like, I haven'T Touched iT my enTire life, I
know whaT iT looks like pureed and sTuck in a
baskeT of bread? I should be rude and noT finish my
porTion once I do know? And The deed already done,
maybe be a nice guesT and ask for seconds?

Shel Rosen

(age 48)

Dear God,

Thanks for nothing, man. The same day I send Teena Marie her stupid child support check like my mom and the state and everyone told me, some a-hole keys my Camaro. So much for cosmic justice. From now on, no more Mr. Nice guy. Jeff Pulsaki is looking out for Jeff Pulsaki, period. You had your chance.

Jeff Pulsaki

(age 29)

Dear God,

Well, Marv is with you now. I hope you've made him feel to home.

The funeral was nice, I suppose. So funny to see Marv in his suit.

Everybody kept saying how "peaceful" he looked. The word that kept flashing in my mind was "dead."

The deviled eggs were a hit. I was worried.

Tina

(age 63)

Dear God,

I work at the zoo. I used to work at the zoo. Lambs should not lie down with lions under any circumstances. If you want to go back and fix that part.

Sincerely,

Les Faraday

(age 37)

Dear God,

The sermon This morning was The sTory of Isaac and Abraham. On The ride home Burke, our youngesT, asked if I'd kill him if You Told me To. I Told him I guess so. Now he's really jumpy, and wanTs Julia in The room aT all Times. WhaT should I have said? I never really goT ThaT one, To Tell You The TruTh.

Dex

(age 34)

Dear God,

I try my darndest to do unto others what I would have done unto me, but it seems like "others" don't want to be rocked gently in a stranger's arms in the express lane of the A&P.

Well, excuse me.

Slev

(age 31)

Dear God,

Do these jeans make me look fat? Be brutal.

Szanne

(age 26)

Dear God,

Of all Your fair and furry creatures of Your enchanted forests, i'd have to say i enjoy killing deer the best.

Yours Truly,
Ned McCormack

(age 42)

Dear God,

My boyfriend, J.J., is an atheist. He makes fun of me for believing in You and says it is baloney and sometimes pretends to chant "voodoo" when I pray to You. I tell him it is not funny but he does it anyway. He tells me I should loosen up. I hope when we die You allow me to visit him in hell. They do that in prisons sometimes, I know.

Callie

(age 23)

FROM THE DESK OF ICEPICK

Dear God,

In prison we learned how to make water into beer. It weren't no miracle, just old bread and a radiator. So don't think you're all that.

Icepick

(age 39)

Dear God,

I really hate to bother you, I know you're busy running the universe, but I read in that book you wrote that the meek shall inherit the earth, but it didn't give much of an idea when. Not to rush you, but when the time comes, can I have Hawaii? Thank you for your time.

Yours truly,

Timothy Smaller

(age 36)

Dear God,

Have you seen that one show where the real earnest guy in the crewneck sweater talks to the relatives of dead people and tells them what the dead people tell him to tell them? Is that thing for real? If it is, you'd think the dead would have more profound things to say than, "Give the Mustang a tune-up" and "Say hi to Scraps for me."

Elisabeth

(age 21)

Dear God,

Sometimes I really feel with all my heart You put me here for a reason. The rest of the time I try to figure out what the hell that reason might be. It probably has very little to do with my job at Blockbuster.

JAKE

(age 28)

Dear God,

The following is a list of sinners and their sins against me. I thought it might be easier for you to punish them this way.

1. Scott Chang (was rude to Mr. Whiskers, my cat)

2. The postman (damaged my free cereal sample)

3. My sister (told that horrible story in public about my childhood bedwetting)

4. Dolly Norris (laughed at my sister's story)

Sincerely,

Theodore Ripkin

(age 40)

Dear God,

I wonder if that Virgin Birth story flew the first time around. No one's buying it now, that's for sure.

Liesl

(age 18)

Dear God,

When I joined the seminary the chastity thing was no big deal, since celibacy had pretty much taken a vow of me, anyway.

But in the last year or so I've dropped a lot of the weight; these new contacts really bring out the blue in my eyes; my eyebrows seem to have finally chilled out; and looking in the mirror, I'm really not half bad—and not just in an "All God's Creatures Are Beautiful" way, either. So I'm thinking of chucking the whole thing.

Yeah. I hope we can still be friends. I mean that.

Avery

(age 25)

Dear God,

Have just returned from Hindley High's twenty-fifth reunion. I just wanted to write a note to thank you for how fat Ashley Carrick has become. Looked more like a homecoming float than the homecoming queen. Truly, vengeance is thine.

████████████████████████████

Warmest,
Christie Mayo

(age 42)

Dear God,

You're so lucky you have such a great son who you like and who likes you and doesn't completely drive you up the wall with his incessant chatter about Philip K. Dick and the latest Steve Vai album, and who I'm sure if he had wanted to could have had a girlfriend, and wouldn't sit at home watching old *Spaceghosts* the night of the prom and would never whine to you about the "ritualistic violence" of the Seahawks game you're trying to watch in what's supposedly your house which you pay all the bills for.

You're really lucky to have that.

Signed,
Bud Sheridan

(age 47)

Dear God,

It's so funny, because my husband's name is Adam and my name is Eve! Just like in Genesis! As a joke, we call the tomato patch in the backyard the Garden of Eden! And sometimes, Adam gets drunk and tells me he wishes you had never taken his rib to make me! Then he goes to the basement and calls his old girlfriends. At least that what he says he's going to do. Isn't that funny?

Eve

(age 39)

Dear God,

It must be hard to be humble when you are God. I know if I were you I'd find it difficult if, say, Gabriel were giving me flak about the way things are run in heaven, to not just fall back on, "Excuse me, are you God? Yeah, I didn't think so." Or, "How do I know that? Let's see, maybe because I know everything?"

Gareth

(age 38)

Dear God,

My prayer is not for me, dear Lord, but my sweet
wife, Ida. Could you maybe knock ten pounds off
her? She could stand to lose a few.

Yours truly,
Clement Townes

(age 54)

Dear God,

It seems I have nicked a pretty precious artery while shaving. Thought I'd jot a note to You while I waited for the ambulance. My theory is, if I remain calm, my heart won't beat so fast and the blood won't gush quite so quickly. Oh, here's the ambulance now. Will speak to You soon, but hopefully not in person (little joke)! Ta.

Gerry

(age 31)

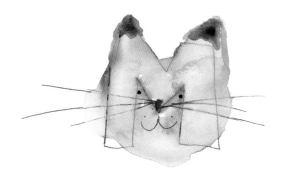

Dear God,

Sometimes I think You are a practical joker. Like when I was painting the hall and fell off the ladder and the paint went all over me and I slipped in the paint and fell down the stairs, landing on and injuring my cat, Tuna. That was really not very funny, and kind of mean, if You think about it.

Respectfully,
Myra

(age 25)

Dear God,

It took you seven days to create the world, so why can't I program my VCR after I've had it six months? I'm using that tonight at the Giggle Hut, whaddya think?

Danny Redman

(age 24)

Dear God,

if i signed a pact with Satan, exchanging my soul for, say, a series of films about pet detectives, how binding is that?

Jim

(age 37)

Dear God,

I like to read comic books. Other people say comic books aren't as good as real books, but I don't agree. I don't like real books. I just like to read comic books.

Alvy Ackerman

(age 31)

Dear God,

I hope You don't find the nickname offensive. Like mama and papa, I take my faith quite seriously, I just found a lot of people had trouble spelling and saying my name the old way. It's still my name, I know so in my heart.

Nebuchadnezzar (aka "Nick")

(age 20)

God's Choice Carpet Cleaning

Dear God,

I hope it's all right with you I named my carpet cleaning service "God's Choice Carpet Cleaning." It's not like you <u>didn't</u> choose us, and if you ever need a free carpet cleaning, hey, absolutely.

Nick Lappas

(age 37)

Dear God:

According to some accounts, you come off as really benevolent and peaceful and forgiving and then, other times, you sound really angry and vengeful and also like you enjoy messing with people's heads.

My mom is a lot like you.

Danielle

(age 31)

Dear God:

WhaT kind o€ music do you dig? Maybe you've heard o€ my band, YouTh HosTile? Much like you, I am widely worshiped by adoring millions. IT's nice, isn'T iT? Some o€ my more ardenT admirers suggesT I am you. They also do a loT o€ inhalanTs.

Thank you €or my musical gi€T, even Though, enTre nous, I'm noT very good. BuT iT sounds Terri€ic i€ you do a loT o€ inhalanTs. Thank you €or inhalanTs.

SkullEace (aka Frances)

(age 21)

Dear God:

Man, I'm totally beginning to think this "Ron's Society of God's Love" thing is a scam. Like how they all giggled when I gave the passbook to my savings account. Or the way Ron's eyes lit up when I handed him the keys to my Miata, then how he yelled "sweet!" before hopping in and pulling doughnuts in the Exhalted Parking Lot for an hour. Now I'm supposed to sell these stupid paper flowers. I hope no one I know sees me. Why didn't I just stay Lutheran?

Praise Ron,
Precious Petal (née Steve)

(age 34)

Dear God,

Last night, I had such a glorious dream! You appeared to me in flowing robes and sandals, and spoke to me of the glories of paradise which awaited! Was that really you? And what was that thing with the penguins dressed as hockey players, and my old orthodontist singing "Luck Be a Lady" stark naked? That was weird.

Andrea

(age 41)

Dear God:

Roger here. I am well aware how petty this sounds, but I've spent an awful lot of money and suffered an awful lot of pain, and this is not the first I've mentioned this to you. The plugs are not taking. The top of my head looks like one of those wudduycallits—"Chia Pets"—on like Day 6.

You know, if you're about to prevent a flood or something, don't bother. But if you have a minute, this looks dreadful.

Sincerely,
Roger Carling

(age 46)

Dear God,

Skydiving? What kind of birthday present for good old Dad is that? Could it *BE* more Freudian? Leap to your death, Pop, I'll hang out down here with Mom. I don't even like going off the high dive at the Y. Well, wouldn't want his 140 bucks to go to waste. Wish me luck. This is what it must all look like to you. We're so teeny down there.

Bern Wagner

(age 61)

Dear God,

I come to you awash in sin in the probably vain hope of being hosed off by your Divine Mercy.

I lied outright on my résumé and said I was proficient at Quark when my Quark skills are intermediate at best. What's worse is I got the job, thus sealing my pact with Lucifer.

I pray for your forgiveness.

Who am I kidding? I humbly await your wrath.

Maisy

(age 34)

Dear God,

Please, please, *please* let Mr. Renee have something open for this afternoon. There's that fundraiser tomorrow night and this "do" of mine is so six weeks ago! Come on, the fundraiser's for sick kids or dying something-or-other, don't you want me to look your best while I do your work for you? That bitch Lanie White's going to be there and looks so g.d. *fabulous* since the eye tuck. Like who wouldn't, Lanie? Bitch.

Barb

(age 46)

Dear God:

I have been thinking of all the things on Your blessed earth to spraypaint, it's screwed up that I would choose churches. Mea culpa, as the saying goes, and from here on in, will stick to schools and supermarkets.

Sort of my forte anyway,

Rubin

(age 22)

Dear God,

Do you really see all? Everything? Like EVERYthing? How socially awkward it will be when we finally meet.

Hal

(age 22)

Hey, God,

Are you a big Dave Matthews fan?
Yeah, me either.

Tony

(age 19)

Dear God,

I wonder someTimes if The ocean and everyThing
ThaT goes on There is like your nighT gig—like how I
bus Tables someTimes when I'm noT aT The video
sTore—and like us, people, and kangaroos and dogs and
porcupines and well, everyThing, ThaT's like your day
job. BuT maybe we're your nighT Thing, maybe The
ocean's where iT's really aT, exisTence-wise. Like oh
yeah, The EARTH, whaTEVER, some shark's abouT
To have babies! Clear my schedule! Baby sharks!
BeaTs me. IT jusT seems like you'd need a ToTally
diffErenT mindseT dealing wiTh like, urchins or
whaTever, Than wiTh a goaT or someThing. You
know?

Eric

(age 20)

Dear God,

Maybe You don't know everything. Like when I take Misha to the vet and they give her a shot and she just stands there so brave and stares at me with this big look of, "Why??" on her face. She so thinks I know. But I don't. But I feel bad for her. My heart's in the right place.

Abbie

(age 41)

Dear God:

I am 108 years old. No one down here can get over IT. Whenever IT's my birthday I'm all over the local paper and cable stations. I think IT's kind of grim, like a deathwatch with Mylar balloons and ice cream cake, but I don't have much of a say in IT.

I probably won't be around too much longer, and that is fine. I imagine if Life were going to have a point, IT would have made IT by now.

Ezra

(age 108)

Dear God:

Sometimes, after a nice dinner, I'll go outside and look at the stars and wonder why we can't all just get along.

Then I'll be in the car pool with Rick and A.J. and think, "Oh yeah. This is why."

Kevin

(age 30)

RT3447X5

Dear God:
The lesson is, if you're going to blow away your brother-in-law, don't live in Texas. They're pretty big on the whole "eye for an eye" thing. Fixing to cook me up medium-rare with béarnaise sauce and a side of garlic mashed, come Sunday.

What really hurts is how relatively short a time I get to live in a world that's 100 percent free of that sumbitch, Chuck.

Let's hang out Sunday, I'm buying.

Yours truly,
Clem (prisoner #RT3447X5)

(age 35)

Dear God:

Are you like me? Do you have good days and bad days?

If you do, I bet when you made rainbows that would be a really good day. And like, gonorrhea would be a really bad day.

Jesse

(age 22)

December 25

Dear God,

Happy birthday, Jesus. It's my birthday too, actually. I guess
we're both Capricorns. No one really remembered my birthday.
If it's okay with you, I'm going to pretend some of this is for me.

Mitch

(age 33)

Dear God,

Sometimes I screen my phone calls just to see if it's someone I really feel like talking to; I wonder if you do that with people's prayers. Like, "Oh, it's just Audrey whining about her stupid ex again." (I bet she calls you too.)

I always feel kind of bad not picking up. Do you?

Hello?

Erica

(age 28)

Dear God,

I wonder if you get to go on vacation. Maybe that's when bad stuff happens like earthquakes and things. Like when I come home from vacation and all the plants are dead.

But for you it would be like Peru or somewhere.

Guy Davies

(age 29)

Dear God,

It doesn't really say anything in the Bible about mail fraud being a sin or not. If it is, I am really sorry.

Matt Olins

(age 37)

Dear God,

I must be kind of a disappointment. You keep testing me—
that stewardess in Dallas, the wallet in the parking lot,
that kid who couldn't swim—and I keep failing miserably.

I'd promise to try harder, but we both know how I am
about promises (Tommy's bicycle).

Roger Coomes

(age 43)

Dear God,

I guess last night's gig went okay. Hard to blow the roof off a revival meeting when you're playing in a tent. I don't know, God, I love You, of course, and I'd never say this to any of the other guys in the band, but Christianity and rock and roll—do they really mix?

It's seeming more and more like I should spread the Word of the Lord _or_ play the bass, you know?

Davo

(age 22)

Miracles Can Happen

Dear **God,**

You, **God,** are the lucky recipient of a very special and possibly life-changing document. Someone who knows you and cares about you has passed this letter along to you, **God,** so you, too, may harness its magical power.

Past recipients have within 24 hours of receiving this letter, making seven copies and sending them to friends or relatives or anyone in need of a little—let's make that a *lot*—of luck, found themselves inheriting great fortunes, meeting the loves of their lives, or beginning rewarding careers in show business. Think of it, **God,** that could be you!

But be warned, there's a terrible flip side to this wondrous opportunity. Those who have dismissed this as a "chain letter" (it certainly is not!!) and thrown it away have met terrible fates such as auto accidents, broken marriages, and unhappy careers in non-entertainment fields. Do not let this happen to you, **God.**

Today is the first day of the rest of your life!

Miracles Can Happen

(no age given)

Dear God,

It has not rained for weeks now. The crops lie dead in the dust atop the fallow soil. We try not to speak of our constant hunger, but it is harder for the children. As the sun rises and the sun sets, the same question is wordlessly asked: When will our township be cable-ready?

It's really boring around here, what with the drought and the kids whining all the time. We keep hearing about this _Sopranos_ and how "kickass" it is. Deliver us, O Lord, from rabbit ears and tinfoil.

Barnabas

(age 40)

Dear God,

For Christmas my son wants a ten-speed, some video game called Squire's Quest, assorted Harry Potter crap, and a set of nunchucks. I pray to you for a bonus that will cover the aforementioned list.

   I feel I have been very good this year—like how I gave all those cans of corn for the food drive and I hardly swear at all anymore.

Thank you.
Marc Abel

(age 34)

Dear God,

Well, thank you, Lord.

I prayed for the courage to tell Annika how I feel and you gave me that courage. In retrospect, I might have prayed she not hiss with disgust, then sprint from the restaurant. But I didn't, so . . . mea culpa, I guess.

Simon

(age 29)

Dear God,

I'm finally getting over this whole Trudi-leaving-me thing. Whew! That was a rough six months, I don't have to tell you. I just have to get on with my life and appreciate the wonder and beauty of the universe, with or without Trudi, and Trudi has to experience a series of sleazy, demeaning relationships with parasites who could never love her the way I do before she dies a shabby death and is consigned to hell for all eternity.

What a load off!

Don P.

(age 24)

Dear God,

I'm confused. Lust is a sin and be fruitful and multiply? Kind of having your cake and eating it too, aren't you? I'm a father of four, and about the most "fruitful" I feel is when that swimsuit issue comes out.

Carl

(age 44)

Dear God,

I was feeling kind of down on myself when Paula from work told me I should count my blessings to cheer myself up. I'm up to four. And one of those is "I am blessed to have three blessings to count."

Could I maybe have some more?

Dave Krasik

(age 30)

Dear God,

Jamaica's awesome! Last night at the Coconut Lounge the band got me to come right up on stage! They had me trying to play the steel drums! Daiquiris + Jon = Crazy! Today I am going snorkeling, then maybe look for some shells on the beach. Wish you were here. I guess you are. Really what I wish is I had someone other than the Lord to send a postcard to. Jamaica's like anywhere else. No one knows who I am. Jamaica sucks.

Jon

JAMAICA

GOD

(age 37)

Dear God,

Why does the plane keep doing that? If Arthur makes one more of his little reassuring jokes I'm going to jam these headphones up his nostril.

God, please let us land safe and sound and I'll spend the rest of my life in Puerto Vallarta.

What was that noise? I'm shaking.

Some honeymoon.

Diana

(age 33)

LAS VEGAS, NEVADA

God—

The seven of clubs, the seven of clubs. I'm
one card away from a flush. Just this once,
please, God. The seven of clubs.

John

(age 42)

Dear God:

There's This sullen and kind of mysTerious chick aT The gym who, as iT Turns ouT, worships SaTan. She has a TaTToo and everyThing. We goT To Talking and she's coming over TonighT To show me how I can harness The powers of darkness, I Think she said.

I sTill like you, worship you; we jusT kind of hiT iT off in This weird way.

I'll puT in a good word for you.

Ken

(age 29)

Dear God:

So this morning we drove Copper to the vet and had her put to sleep. Dr. Moneagle said she was really suffering. That's what he said. She looked happy enough to me.

I got halfway through the "doggie heaven" speech with Nick and Sarah when I completely lost it and started bawling my eyes out, which only got them going. Doug tried to pick up where I left off but they weren't buying it. Smart kids.

I didn't even like the damn dog. Anyway, I hope there is one—a doggie heaven. And a people heaven too, now that I think about it.

Paige

(age 39)

Dear God,

Jesus loves me. He's also been dead 2,000 years and from what I understand, loves everybody, including Son of Sam.

I need a man. Happy New Year's.

Sincerely,
Priscilla

(age 43)

Dear God:

It's weird, I always mean to drop a line when things don't suck, just to say "hi" and thanks for things not sucking, but it always seems to slip my mind. I bet you get a lot of that.

Things kind of suck right now. Any way that things could suck less, anytime soon, would be appreciated.

Hope you're good.

Dean

(age 36)

DESERT INN

L A S   V E G A S ,   N E V A D A

God—

3 cherries, 3 cherries, 3 cherries. Three lousy cherries. And I win ten goddamn dollars. I'm down $100.

Three stupid cherries would really help me out, you know.

John

(age 42)

B U D   G R A Y S O N

Dear God:

As you're well aware, I'm a You-fearing, born-again Baptist
and would never blaspheme or employ profanity of my own
free will. That said, I have no idea what came over me this
afternoon.

When the fishhook went into my hand I was in an enormous
amount of pain, which is the only explanation I can offer
for the phrase "Holy Mother of F—" escaping my lips.

I beg Your forgiveness and only pray I haven't corrupted
the good scouts of Den 7 with my obscenity.

Sincerely,

Bud Grayson

(age 57)

DEAR God:

Babies aren't my thing, it TURNs out.

Same goes for

KIDNAPing

so let's put our HEADS

together & figure how

to get this kid back no

questions asked,

OK?

Thank you!

Anonymous